EDDIE:
ONE DOG'S JOURNEY FROM
HOBO TO A HOME

EDDIE: ONE DOG'S JOURNEY FROM HOBO TO A HOME

STACEY DEXTER

Sanctuary Stories

For Samantha...I love you always xoxoxo

And to Steve and Judy Davis:
Thank you for loving Eddie

PREFACE

If anyone had told me that one day, I'd be writing a story about my dog Eddie, I would have laughed and said something like, "Yeah, that's just what the world needs—another dog story." (Eye-roll, big sigh.) But when the Universe plunked Eddie down in my path, there was no ignoring this unusual creature. Any dog lover will tell you that their dog is *the* best, *the* smartest, *the* cutest, and of course, the star of the most hilarious stories. Just look on YouTube, Facebook, Twitter, Instagram; we love our pets. We've got it bad. I would say that we sometimes prefer them to children. Humans have even created social media accounts for their pets. There are dogs that have more followers than celebrities. Their likability is universal, their innocence pure. Eddie has his own unique story, and it unfolded long before the internet gave humans a way to tell of their pets' every wag and walk. Eddie did not wear outfits, and he most definitely wasn't carried around in a purse.

Dogs have always been a part of my life and I love them, no matter the breed. My Grammie Dexter always had three or four dogs, all different types. There was Bourbon, the cagey, black Lab mix; Governor, the messy, drooling basset hound; Missy, the beagle mix with a huge benign tumor on her side; and Canus, the doltish yellow Lab. A gigantic St. Bernard named Chief lived across the street from my grandmother's house, and he and Bourbon would go at it like mortal enemies. Grammie would then come out of the house, grab the garden hose, and blast it at them to stop them from killing each other. Thrilling! In my immediate family, we didn't have a dog until I was around fourteen, but they were everywhere in my neighborhood, and our friends usually had them, too.

Whenever I am out and see a dog approaching, I speak to them as if I've known them all of our lives. "Hiiiii there, angel (or cutie or handsome or luv-bug)! How are you doing today?" I briefly nod and say a quick hello to the human with them, my focus squarely on the dog.

I love them, even if we are strangers. My love affair with dogs has been going on my entire life, and I don't see that changing.

Today, we often give our pets people names and a voice so we can relate to them on *our* level. In my case, that voice sometimes comes with an accent. One of my dogs was a greyhound who had originated from a Florida racetrack, so her "voice" had a sweet, Southern twang. I enjoy playing ventriloquist for my dogs, letting the canine-challenged humans who can't "speak dog" know their food preferences, favorite resting spot, enemies, and neuroses.

In my imagination, Eddie's voice was that of a tough biker dude, with a soft center. His sentences were clipped and pointed. No screwing around. He was a dog of few words. After years of having various types of dogs from mutts to retired racing greyhounds, Eddie's story has remained the most striking and one that had to be told. From his humble hobo beginnings to his quirky adventures, Eddie is one for the books.

I miss you, Ed. XO

1

It is important to start at the beginning and explain the Nikki-to-Eddie transformation. Nikki appeared one summer in the early 1990s in our small seaside tourist town of Rockport, Massachusetts. I was living there with my daughter, Sam, then-husband, Frank, and our greyhound/shepherd mix, Wolfie. We were your typical family, busy all the time, running here and there. In the months of May and June, the large number of vacation homes in our area brought an increase in local traffic, shiny new beach chairs, extra family and friends, and a few summer dogs to join the natives. You could smell the barbecued chicken and hot dogs starting in early June.

Back then there wasn't a leash law, so dogs freely roamed the streets. Each summer, different dogs would show up with their families, just like Nikki did that one sunny, Saturday afternoon. Nikki was a husky mix with a lop-sided grin. He looked somewhat wolf-like and cool, as if he had just ridden into town on a Harley. All he needed was an earring pierced through his left ear and a red bandanna. Wolfie took to him immediately. She was so easygoing, and he was a charmer with that smile of his. From that first morning that he appeared in the neighborhood, Wolfie and Nikki became BFFs. Each day when I let Wolfie out to relieve herself, there he'd be, waiting to escort her to their favorite pee spot on the back lawn.

Some investigative and observational skills were needed to know who this dog was, cozying up to my Wolfie. Nikki wasn't overly friendly to humans, and it took some trickery to get close enough to check out his dog tags. I devised a plan to lure him to me with some deliciously greasy Oscar Mayer baloney. No dog I knew could resist it. He was hypnotized by the pork waving at him, his nose twitching, taking in the smell. While he chomped on the bait, I lightly grasped his collar, rotating it to reveal a recent rabies tag and the name "Nikki" before he wiggled out of my grasp.

He wasn't emaciated and appeared to be in decent shape. I guessed his weight to be about fifty pounds and his age approximately five years old, though I really had no idea.

Nikki was neutered and seemed harmless. His beat-up red collar and tags suggested ownership, though his fur was a little grimy. He could've used a good bath. His gray, white, and black coat complemented his fluffy husky/shepherd-mix tail, but his garbage breath could stop a truck. One whiff of that mix of rotten fish and coffee grounds, and I found myself cursing his owners, wondering why he hadn't been to the doggie dentist. Yikes. He wasn't the least bit aggressive, just not the touchy-feely type. He didn't lean into me or want to have a cuddle. I tried to look him in the eyes, but he ducked his head. He just wanted the baloney, thank you, and then, goodbye!

In that moment, there was no cause for alarm. I approved of Wolfie's new buddy. He was another one of the many dogs that would come and go with the season. I didn't think much of seeing any dog out and about in the neighborhood. It was summertime and life was moving at an accelerated pace. People were frantic to cram in as much fun as possible during their vacations, and my family wasn't any different. I accepted that he was one of our transient summer visitors and returned to my busy life.

I had a lot to learn about my new friend.

2

We couldn't get too close to Nikki for the first few months; he'd shy away if you reached out to pet him and kept his distance. Initially, Nikki was only friendly with our retired neighbor, Steve, allowing him to pat him. He even went into Steve's house. I was a little jealous; Nikki was spending all his free time with our girl Wolfie, so couldn't he be a bit more cordial? His manners were below average. But I was so swamped with my job and my life that I didn't have a lot of time to dwell on how I felt about Nikki. I was working full-time and raising a busy student-athlete. I didn't stop long enough to form much of a bond with him, other than saying hello to him each day with a smile in my voice.

I felt that he at least trusted me a little bit since he came to our door every morning to pick up Wolfie for their daily adventures. Dogs are transparent like that: no foolish human mind games. He would give me the equivalent of a dude's head nod as they trotted off the porch together, blinking a wink at me with his husky blue eyes. I started to see why Wolfie was enamored; he was charming. His personality was intriguing. Who was this dog?

The summer progressed, hot and busy with lots of activity, and Nikki was always present, hanging out with Wolfie or Steve. He'd lie in the backyard, under the shade of the oak trees, panting in the humid air. He did not want to be inside, always preferring to be out. He gradually became a little less shy, a little more trusting. My family and I were now "allowed" to pet him and feed him treats. He occasionally came inside our home, only to scoot out after a short visit. He always seemed a little nervous inside the house, ready to bolt, hyper-alert. My mind said PTSD, but why?

In late August, we noticed that most of the summer people had started to depart, and one by one the part-time dogs were going back home. Doggie summer camp was coming to an end––but Nikki never left. His routine never changed. He was still content spending his days between our yard and Steve's. Slowly, I became aware that he was living under Steve's back porch. If anyone was looking for Nikki, that's where he'd be, tucked under the stairs. Had he been abandoned? Forgotten? Who and where were his owners?

I realized that we knew little about Nikki. He had fallen through the cracks of backyard barbecues, beach time, and summer vacations. We had failed to notice that a runaway was in the neighborhood. Nikki was no dummy. He had us all fooled. He was the shrewdest doggie scam artist ever, trotting through the streets, keeping his head down, flying under the radar. He had perfected his image as a beach bum, a seasonal chum, a part-time sidekick with a secret. He had no one.

3

I clearly remember the day Hurricane Edouard invited himself to Rockport. Edouard was a volatile Category 4 storm of Cape Verdean descent that had traveled from the tip of Africa over the toasty-warm Caribbean waters before heading toward the United States. He was locked and loaded, a colossal bully coming to wreck the end of that particular Labor Day weekend. Our local barbecues and parties had all been canceled. Patio furniture was tied down and covered with tarps. A heavy cloud of depression hung in the air along with the storm, the humidity an unwanted winter coat. Edouard crashed the party like a belligerent drunk; everyone braced for his imminent arrival, this unwanted interloper.

As with any hurricane, we were aware of the potential power loss, the street flooding, the menacing winds. I was grateful to be inside. It was raining so violently, it was as if storm vandals were throwing buckets of water at the house, one after the other, in gleeful succession. It was unrelenting. I looked out of the kitchen window into Steve's backyard and, lo and behold, there was Nikki, huddled under the porch. Why wasn't he at home? I wasn't going to leave him out there. I knew he was shy. I knew it wouldn't be easy. But it would be cruel not to try. He was a defenseless animal that needed my help. My fury increased, thinking of the irresponsibility of his owners, my anger thrusting me into action.

I grabbed the keys to the truck, a jacket, and an old towel. I yelled to Frank that I was headed out to pick up Nikki by way of Steve's driveway. There was no offer of help. Even though our yards were connected, there was no way that I was going to attempt to make it across the property on foot to get to him. I needed the protection of the truck. The trees were whipping around like ribbons on a stick, the wind hostile and unpredictable. My heart was pounding.

This was a serious dog rescue, and I was determined to get him to safety. I felt like a superhero, the drama of the situation fueling my adrenaline. I was going to save Nikki.

4

This was the strongest storm of the 1996 season, and it had been backhanding the Massachusetts coastline for hours. As I was pulling around to Steve's driveway, I started to realize that we never saw anyone with Nikki. No one calling his name or looking for him. I was wondering if he even had a home. I was starting to feel like such a dope! Had we missed the signs of abandonment? Throughout the summer, we had tried to lure him into our home to have a sleepover with Wolfie, but he never took the bait. I had attributed his actions to some form of loyalty to his real masters, but now I was rethinking my theory. He was slippery and cunning. I would have a dog biscuit or some hamburger to seduce him inside, but he would quickly scoot in, snatch the snack, and take off running like a thief, greasy drool clinging to his whiskers. He acted like an escaped convict. Did he view a home with humans as a prison? My thoughts ran amok, processing the events of the last few months. *Focus, Stacey. Nikki needs you.* I pulled into Steve's, took a deep breath, and sprang out of the truck, jumping through huge puddles that were already loaded with debris and mud across the lawn.

"Get in the car *now!*" I hollered at Nikki, pointing toward the truck. I was probably scaring the crap out of him.

My voice could hardly be heard over the groaning of the wind, swollen with the weight of rain. I was getting soaked standing in the yard, pleading for Nikki to come out from under his hideout. I could feel his resistance to leaving his safe haven under Steve's back porch.

He tried not to make eye contact and pushed his body further under the steps. He really didn't want to go. He didn't want to get too close. But in that moment, at the height of the storm, even Nikki seemed to sense that I was his best option for survival.

It is in times like this that it frustrates me the most that humans and dogs cannot communicate in the same language. Nikki was like a puzzle, a story to be assembled piece by piece.

I couldn't reason with him, so I had to lead him out from under the porch, across the muddy wet lawn, and into Steve's driveway. I knelt down under the stairs and took him gently by the collar. He dragged his feet like a toddler. As I shepherded him into my truck, hoisting his stiff back legs into the passenger seat, he looked at me dejectedly, as if I were Tommy Lee Jones in *The Fugitive,* and he had just been captured after years on the run. "I just saved you from the storm," I reasoned as I draped the towel around him. "You should be grateful."

I kissed his wet nose. He looked miserable, his ears flat and dripping. He was shivering with cold, scared and probably hungry, but he came home with me and our adventures with Nikki/Eddie began.

5

Once inside, with Nikki dry and snuggled up to Wolfie on her bed, I gently removed Nikki's collar and studied the tags. I called the number on the ID and was surprised when it connected me to an animal shelter in the Boston area. I explained that I had Nikki with me in Rockport and that he had been in our neighborhood all summer. Could she help me find his owner?

"Owner!" she exclaimed as she clicked through her files. "Nikki was adopted by a family in Newburyport in the spring. Where is he right now?"

"Under my dining room table, with my dog, Wolfie," I replied. Nikki peeked at me with one eye, quickly closing it as if feigning sleep.

"You're kidding!" said the clerk. *Why was this so difficult to believe? What was this dog's story?*

The clerk began to disclose the details. Nikki had been adopted several times in the last few years, only to run away each time. He always ended up back at the shelter.

"Can't you keep him?" she asked.

Keep him?! "Oh, I don't know..." I replied lamely. She pleaded with me. "You don't understand. Nikki's never stayed with anyone. He's been so hard to place." *Oh, crap.* The guilt was upon me as I slapped my forehead, wishing I had never made this phone call.

"We think he was abused early on (I started to soften) because he scares easily (melting), and no one's been willing to help him through the transition from shelter dog to beloved pet. He must like you and your dog. Couldn't you just keep him?" *Oh boy. How could I say no to this poor lost lamb?* I was a goner.

I glanced over at Nikki. I swear he was using all his acting skills, looking unfazed and bored yet listening to every word. I peered over at my husband, who just shrugged.

"Well, I guess we can try," I said.

As I hung up the phone, Nikki and Wolfie looked up at me. Their doggy faces were full of hope and love. The tenderness slayed me into acceptance. We all had come to understand that Nikki had street smarts and took care of himself. He was feeding himself somehow since he wasn't underweight. We knew from observing him over the summer that he preferred to be outside, all the time, in any weather. Nikki had decided to trust me, and I didn't want to let him down.

However, he was uneducated about what it meant to be part of a family, to have most of his needs met by humans and to obey certain rules. I laugh now at how uneducated we were about *him.* He had his own rules, and obeying humans wasn't his forte. According to what little info we received from the shelter, he had essentially lived without ownership for a long time. He was a certified hobo. I was intrigued by him. I had to know more. Who was this "Nikki"?

A decision had to be made. I declared that our new dog (and free, what a bonus!) did not look like a "Nikki" and needed a fresh start. I had named Wolfie after Wolfgang Amadeus Mozart (I am a musician), so we felt that Nikki should have an "important" name, too. From then on, he was known as Eddie, named after that impressive hurricane.

Eddie was now to be sheltered from all storms; he had a new family and wouldn't be alone in this world anymore. We bestowed upon him his very own sleeping blanket, some bowls from the cupboard for food and water, and that day he moved in for good.

Wolfie, left with Eddie

Woolfie and Eddie
Author

6

Eddie settled in and, with Wolfie by his side, romped through September, enjoying the cooler weather. By now he had received multiple brushings but few baths. Wolfie's fur was short and easy to manage. But for rock-and-roll boy, we had to call in the dog grooming professionals; Eddie's thick, messy mane and his distaste for bathing was too much of a challenge for me and the garden hose. I only had to walk over near the hose and he would take off. But once he was professionally buffed and fluffed, he was a beauty—his black, gray, and white fur like a wolf's.

Except for that nasty breath, he was a looker. Wolfie didn't seem to mind his poor dental hygiene as much as we did; she had sniffed a lot of butts in her day, so what was a little bad breath? Next stop was the veterinarian for a full checkup. We knew that he had received a shot for rabies because of his tags, but little else. After having him a few weeks, we tried to contact the shelter in Boston for more information about his care, but oddly enough, their number had been disconnected. *Hmmmm—was having Eddie enter our lives some form of divine intervention? Why had he been put in my path?*

Our vet's office had been through a few personnel changes, so I booked Eddie with a new female veterinarian. She seemed pleasant enough, though I could see by the look on Eddie's face that his nervousness was going to be an issue. Frank and I tried distracting him with soothing petting and chitchat, to no avail. The anxiety of the visit led Eddie into a spiral of heavy panting (cue the icky breath) and nonstop flatulence. If you place three adults with one petrified dog crammed elbow to paw in a tiny exam room no bigger than a jail cell, you get room-clearing dog farts. This was not amusing for anyone, especially Eddie. He seemed embarrassed; his head hung in shame. His tail was tucked far beneath his belly, and eye contact was minimal. *Does he think that we are here to give him away?*

I hugged him fiercely, breathing through my mouth while the vet examined him. She listened to his heart, checked his eyes and ears, and took a sample of blood. Mercifully, we were out of that exam room in about twenty minutes. We were sent to the waiting room to await the test results. The room was fumigated, and the next patient, a fluffy glamorous poodle, was ushered in. I swear she looked back at Eddie just as the exam room door closed and gave him the dirtiest look. Any chance that he might have had to sniff her butt was *over*.

After about thirty minutes, we were told that his blood work would take at least twenty-four hours to confirm whether Eddie had been exposed to heartworm, a deadly disease in dogs. I was told that even though the test wasn't completed, we could start him on the heartworm medication anyway. He had lived with different owners off and on and had probably been given the medication before so they didn't seem too concerned about his risk. I was a little skeptical, but took the veterinarian's advice, popped out a pill, and gave it to him on the spot. We left with expensive meds, a dazed Eddie, and a lighter wallet. We were all relieved to get out of there. So much for our "free" dog.

On the way home, I was feeling the emotional and financial burden of taking on another dog, especially one with some potentially expensive health issues. But my fear dropped away just looking at Eddie's sweet face. He was with us for a reason. The Universe was at work here, quietly and gently placing Eddie at our door. As we drove back to Rockport, we had the windows wide open because of Eddie's anxiety-produced aroma. Soon, his terror had subsided, and he was fast asleep in the back of the truck, limp from the experience.

7

Soon the evening routine was in full swing and we had put the doctor's visit out of our thoughts. It was time to concentrate on dinner, homework, laundry, and everyone's plans for the night. The dogs had already been walked and fed and were now snoozing on their beds in the living room.

At approximately 8:00 p.m., I was cleaning up the kitchen when I heard one of the dogs panting. My husband had gone out for the evening, and my daughter was at hockey practice. I went into the dining room to investigate and observed Eddie panting in a way that was not normal. He seemed distressed, his eyes glassy and tight. I had always been taught that a panting dog, unless overheated or winded from exertion, was a dog in pain.

Having no idea what was wrong, I quickly called the emergency vet office in Woburn, about an hour away. This was my only option since our vet's office was strictly 9:00 a.m. to 5:00 p.m. The technician advised me to get him up there, pronto. After learning the details of Eddie's earlier vet visit, they felt that he was having a reaction to the heartworm medication and that he could go into cardiac arrest. *What?!*

This was in the 1990s—before we all had cell phones—so I was on my own. The situation was urgent. Was Eddie going to die, just when we had "rescued" him? I looked at Wolfie standing in the doorway, stricken in her own way. She could smell the fear. I couldn't take her with me; it was too stressful. "Okay, boy. Let's go," I instructed Eddie.

"Pant, pant, pant," was his reply. His eyes were a mix of distress and possibly pain. I scrambled outside to my car, pulled up to the front door, and carried Eddie down the steps so that he wouldn't further strain his heart. My heart was squeezing itself in fear and the burden of lifting a fifty-pound dog. I placed him into the back seat with an unsteady, "It's going to be okay, boy. Don't worry."

My acting skills were not as perfected as his were. I was telling him not to be worried, but I was petrified. I tore out of Rockport, and once I hit the highway, I was flying between seventy and eighty miles per hour––this was an emergency! I kept reaching into the back seat to pat and reassure Eddie, praying that I would make it in time. It was so crazy; I was driving like a mother with her sick child in the back seat.

I made it to Woburn in thirty-five minutes. I ran with Eddie in my arms to the reception desk. We were both panting now. I explained that I had just called about Eddie, so the tech came out from the back, snatched him from me, and told me to stay in the waiting room. It was torture. I asked to use the phone and got a hold of my husband, giving him the details between my tears and the shortness of breath that I felt from the fear. "They think that he could be having a reaction to the heartworm medication!" I told him. *I knew we shouldn't have trusted that inexperienced vet!* I felt guilty and stupid, helpless, and confused.

I couldn't understand what the hell had happened with the medication, but I was going to find out. I was attached to him in a way that only true dog lovers can understand. We had only had him for a few weeks, but he was ours. Eddie had become an official, beloved member of our family. He was Wolfie's new brother and doggie buddy. He was neighbor Steve's new sidekick. His story was just beginning, and I couldn't fathom that this could be the end. He had to make it.

After an agonizing hour, the tech appeared—but without Eddie. "We will have to keep him overnight," he explained. "The medication that he was given should not have been administered to him before a definitive diagnosis of heartworm. It's a bad idea to risk it." I was astonished. Eddie was positive for heartworm disease.

"But the vet," I sputtered, "she said...she said that it would be all right even though we didn't know for sure!" I was fuming. "You mean to tell me that we shouldn't have given him that medicine and the vet is at fault?"

The tech nodded his head slightly, maybe not wanting to condemn the veterinarian and instead presenting a professional show of solidarity. Then, to calm me, he said, "Do you want to see him?" *Nice redirection.*

My defenseless boy Eddie had gone through all of this because of a careless mistake. I followed the tech around the desk and back into the inner sanctum of the animal hospital to see him. Eddie was in a large cage, hooked up to an IV, a swollen bag loaded with medicine to counteract the heartworm drug. Thick blue medical tape was wrapped around one of his front legs to hold the needle in place. His paw had been shaved. This was just too much. He looked pathetic, but at least he was safe. I kissed his head and left momentarily to retrieve his blanket from the car for his overnight stay. I wanted to reassure him that I was coming back, but how could I do that?

I hated to leave him but felt he was in good hands. I told him repeatedly that I would be back to get him, desperate to convince him that he was not being abandoned...again. I didn't know if he could understand what I was telling him, but I had to believe that he could, at least intuitively. Our communication had to come within that special sphere of trust: my tone, my presence, my hands running softly over his fur, whispering my love to him into his furry ears.

I left with a heavy heart but also a smoldering rage toward the veterinarian who had treated him incorrectly, almost killing him. She would be hearing from me in the morning. Eddie hadn't had anyone in his corner until now, and I wasn't going to let him down. I was on a mission, and justice for Eddie was at the top of my list.

8

The next day's phone call to the veterinarian's office did not go well. We were told that it was an "honest mistake" made by an inexperienced vet and that they were glad that Eddie was going to be okay. *Well, wasn't that nice of them to be so concerned?* Their nonchalant attitude was rather bizarre. Had this happened before with other patients?

"Gee, thanks," I said, my tone laced with sarcasm, "but we'd like a refund of our entire visit, the medication, and our emergency room visit." Unbeknownst to them, I was holding my fiery tongue, which was ready to go rogue with obscenities. I went on to tell them of my harrowing evening, the race to the emergency vet's office in Woburn, worried to pieces that Eddie could die. There was silence, then whispering. I was put on hold.

A technician eventually came on the line and explained that, indeed, the blood tests showed that Eddie had heartworm and he would need to be treated for it immediately. For six weeks, the treatment would include special medication (arsenic!) and limited time outdoors, except for bathroom breaks. If an infected mosquito (that insufferable carrier of the virus) bit him while he was on the medication, he could die. *What? Our "hobo dog" needed to be quarantined? Oh, that was going to be fun.* Had these idiots not absorbed everything that I had just told them? It was as if they hadn't heard me tell them of the anxiety of the previous night, the exorbitant cost, and *their* veterinarian's huge mistake. I was beyond exasperated.

"I don't feel it's appropriate for your office to handle his treatment *nor* am I comfortable paying you for it. I'd like to speak to the owner of the practice." More *umms* and whispering, and could I please hold another moment?

My indignation was obvious, my temper now on a medium boil. I was trying to control myself with thoughts of *"You get more with honey..."* but it was almost impossible.

Another office person came onto the phone to inform me that Dr. "I Don't Know How to Hire Qualified Employees" wasn't available and that a message would be given to him. Of course, he wasn't available

"If we do not hear from him today, my husband will be calling and you do *not* want to have to deal with *him*," I said in an ominous tone. (Frank was not one to confront anyone, but they didn't know that and I knew that it was possible that the threat of a man calling might help. Ha.) Undaunted by my threat, we didn't receive a call back. *Brazen.* My forgiveness meter plummeted to zero.

The next day Frank called and asked to have the owner brought to the phone. He was told that the doctor would be right with him. My thoughts churned, disappointed that a male caller received their attention right away. I had built up his fierceness, so I put my pride away and let my husband do the talking for us. Frank began slowly and deliberately. "Do you mean to tell me that a mistake made by an employee of your office will not be compensated? Should we be talking to a lawyer instead?" Frank pulled out the lawyer card right out of the gate. *You tell 'em, Frank.*

Even though my husband did not show his anger very often, when he did, he sounded pretty darn scary. Dr. Clueless explained how sorry he was (wah, wah, wah), but he could not refund our money or pay for the emergency care. My husband finally wore him down to agree to treat Eddie for the heartworm at no charge, with free medication, follow-up visits, etc. Something was better than nothing, and this treatment would be expensive and laborious.

As much as our faith in their abilities had deteriorated, we knew that going to another vet would cost us even more money to have Eddie re-evaluated. We decided to go ahead with the treatment, but only under the supervision of one of their more experienced vets. This request was nonnegotiable.

There was never an apology from the original vet that had treated Eddie, and she was conveniently unavailable for our repeated phone calls. *Coward.* Eddie spent the next six weeks confined to our home; his freedom curtailed. We knew that it was in his best interest and temporary, but the look in Eddie's eyes, day after day, seemed to say, "You are just like all of the other humans––jailers!"

I felt like I had tricked him into the world of pet ownership. He was very unhappy. He actually moped—head hanging, eyes averted. He didn't eat much, pushing his food around in his bowl and ignoring treats. I knew depression when I saw it. He stared at the front door most of the day, fixated on the doorknob, as if planning an escape. He wouldn't look at me. The guilt trip was painful. He was missing his daily jaunts to Steve's, wandering the neighborhood, smelling every clue left by another dog, and being his own boss. The look of dejection on his face when I clicked the leash onto his collar to take him out was akin to defeat. *A leash!* Bondage was not the least bit sexy to Eddie. I think he was second-guessing his decision to let us adopt him. Wolfie was a homebody, so at least he had company during his long days of confinement. This was a small salve that I hoped would soften his disappointment in me.

Lesson learned the hard way: don't give a dog a preventative heart-worm pill without first knowing if he is infected. After Eddie's treatment plan was concluded and he was cleared, we never went back to that office again. We often lamented our situation (*should we sue?*), but after careful thought and the fact that Eddie was alive, we dropped it.

We chose our next vet very carefully going forward. Our dogs are family. Choose wisely, dear readers, and learn from me. Our pets are worthy of careful and close selection of their caregivers, especially those outside of the family.

9

After the six weeks of treatment were finally over, Eddie was released from his time in bondage. I was concerned that once he had his freedom back, he may take off for good. After letting Eddie and Wolfie out the door that first morning, I just prayed that the time he had spent indoors may have shown him our true intentions, which were only to love and protect him—not to hold him hostage. He was still "free," just in a different way. Our educations with each other had just begun, and we all had a lot to learn.

Perhaps to convince us that he had succumbed to our efforts to brainwash him into becoming a regular dog, he started to adhere to our rules about mealtime, curfew, and hygiene. He came when called, ate his meals, stayed out of trouble, and kept fairly clean. However, his personality was too strong to be harnessed for long. The real Eddie could not be quashed. Soon he was back to his old tricks of disappearing when called, only to be discovered lying in a bed of leaves in a tucked-away corner of the yard. He loved making his nests of leaves, shaped like a donut, and surrounding him on all sides. It was as if he had created his own womb.

He also began digging holes in the dirt under Steve's porch to lie in, stealing blankets off the neighbors' clotheslines (for extra padding when there weren't any leaves), and being a little bit of a nuisance. He was a tenacious, creative survivor. A world-class hobo dog. My dad used to fondly refer to him as Eddie the Brick, incorrectly suggesting that his blank stare meant he was a bit challenged in the brain department. Au contraire—he was a very clever boy.

Eddie's favorite pastime was being let outside and staying outside for as long as possible, all four seasons. This took some getting used to, as I liked to coddle my pets a little and not have them gallivanting in the neighborhood in the heat, cold, or middle of the night.

Eddie's happiness seemed to depend on this way of life, and even though we didn't completely give in to his demands (he had to come inside during any extreme weather and overnight), we acquiesced a bit to insure his good mood. Eddie had essentially been homeless for years and had learned a thing or two about how to survive without an owner. We had to respect him and his street smarts. Any attempt to control him was a bit laughable. We began to accept him for who he was and just hoped that his "ideas" wouldn't get him into any real trouble.

10

One day our eighty-year-old neighbor, Ginny, wandered over from across the street and into our backyard. I was in the kitchen and happened to spot her heading over to our small back steps. Before I could get to the door, I saw her bend down and scoop up a small blue bowl and start back to her house. I called out to her from the back door. "Hi, Ginny. What's up?" My tone sounded cheery, but my thoughts said *uh-oh*.

"Oh, just gettin' my cat bowl from your steps." *Huh?*

"What do you mean, Ginny? How did it get over here?" *Eddie.*

"Oh, every other day or so, Eddie steals my cats' food bowl and brings it over to your back steps to eat whatever's in it. When I can't find it, I just walk over here and get it. No big deal." I was feeling like I had a kid who stole her kids' lunch money!

"I'm so sorry, Ginny! We just adopted him, and he's still adapting to having someone feed him versus foraging for his own food."

"That's all right," she said, giving me a backhanded wave as she crossed the street. "I think it's funny!" *Whew.* I was grateful for her generous nature and thanked the Universe that Ginny was a true animal lover...because it happened again and again.

I kept an eye out for that little blue bowl for a while, hoping that Eddie wouldn't continue to feel the need to snatch it. My little Oliver Twist, dear fellow. His survival instincts were strong. He eventually stopped stealing the bowl, but he was still his true hobo self, deep down.

11

Thanksgiving was upon us in no time, and we made sure that Eddie was going to enjoy it. He and Wolfie both received turkey bits, mashed potatoes, gravy, and a little pumpkin pie. It was so adorable to watch my two dogs slumbering off into a turkey coma like the rest of us. It was a great day. It felt so good to give love and attention to Eddie, our newest family member. My dad had warmed to him, talking to him like he was a long-lost friend, petting him all afternoon. It was one of the first times I had hosted Thanksgiving, and I was so grateful for the camaraderie. Even my mother was in a rare, upbeat mood. The holiday was a success.

The day after Thanksgiving was a day off from work, but not a day off from yard work. It was a typical New England day, blustery and sunny. Many of our neighbors were outside tidying up their yards, preparing for the winter ahead. We were raking leaves and sweeping debris, and the dogs were out with us. Wolfie stayed close by, but Eddie wandered off, per usual. About an hour had passed when I looked up to see a turkey carcass "walking" along the sidewalk. An entire picked-to-the-bone turkey carcass was making its way toward me carried by none other than Eddie. He had the entire bird in his mouth, covering his head, creating what looked like a turkey skeleton with a dog body. It looked like it had once been a twenty-five-pounder!

"Eddie Dexter!" The body stopped short. The head plopped to the ground. The turkey had obviously been dug out of someone's trash. You should have seen his face. It was covered in congealed turkey fat, light and dark meat, giblets, and bits of stuffing. He sprinted from the bird with a frantic look in his eye, as if he was running from the cops, looking over his shoulder as he rounded the next corner and out of sight.

I only wish I had owned a video camera that day. We all fell about the yard, wailing with laughter, holding onto our sides, rolling in the leaves. Even Wolfie started jumping into the downward dog play stance, barking at us, as if she were laughing, too.

Eddie was just bringing home some leftovers. What a dog. I took a plastic bag out to the sidewalk and quickly stuffed the carcass inside to hide the evidence. It was so gross.

Later that night, he came creeping back home. His shame could not be denied. We had to clean off the turkey garbage that remained stuck to his face. I wet a towel in warm water to wipe him off, and he pulled away like a toddler as I tried to clean off the gunk. In his own way, we liked to think that he was trying to be a contributing member of the family. Eddie seemed to want to pull his own weight. His hijinks and shenanigans had only begun––our family was in for quite a ride. He was such a character. We often wondered if we could teach him how to bring home money...

12

November blew into December, and we were determined that both dogs would have an enjoyable Christmas. We got a kick out of draping Eddie and Wolfie in tinsel and leftover bows and ribbons. Eddie didn't seem to mind all of the extra people in the house; family came and went throughout the day. The abundance of food was a bonus for both dogs. My dad made sure that there were always some tidbits for them—a piece of turkey here, a lick of stuffing there, just enough to make the dogs feel a part of the festivities. Plain old dog food would just not do. Not today.

We always made Christmas stockings with doggie treats and stuffed animals. They both loved tearing into the packages of toys (which we had wrapped individually, just for fun), tossing them around, ripping the heads off of their stuffed kitty-cats or life-like snakes. The sounds of squeaky innards draining from their lifeless, cotton-filled bodies seemed to make each dog feel that they had won some ferocious battle. They both panted and smiled their doggy grins the entire day, satisfied with their kill.

After a few hours of Christmas joy, Eddie ached to go outside. He would disappear from the living room and stand patiently by the front door, waiting for someone to come along and open it. He would never lie down by the door—he'd just stand there, like a sentry, panting with the anticipation of his next adventure. Even though his favorite people and plenty of goodies were inside the house, he craved the outdoors. Unless the temperature dropped below freezing or it was snowing heavily, out he'd go, en route to Steve's and/or parts unknown.

There wasn't a leash law in Rockport in the 1990s, so most dogs freely roamed the neighborhood. Reflecting back on those times, I wouldn't be so liberal today with my "let them be free" attitude.

13

As the winter months slowly ticked by, our family, including our dogs, fell into a routine. My daughter, Sam, was in school all day, followed by many hours of ice hockey practice. Frank and I both worked full-time, so we were out the door by eight and not back until five or six o'clock. If the weather was on the mild side, Eddie would be let out for the day to satisfy his innate need to wander the streets. After Wolfie's morning duties, she'd hop up onto my bed to nest, content to snuggle into the warmth of the down comforter. She had no desire to spend the day outside in the cold.

Steve was retired and home most days, so we knew that this was where Eddie ended up for the majority of the daylight hours. Occasionally, I would call Steve from work to touch base, to see if he had seen Eddie that day. "Oh yeah," he'd reply, chuckling, "been here all morning helping me shovel." I could hear the smile in Steve's voice, and I was grateful that Eddie had his own human buddy whom I could check in with at any time.

If the temperature took a dive, Steve would bring Eddie into his home. Steve's wife, Judy, would usually be there too, and they'd watch some TV until one of us returned from work. Eddie would munch on a few extra dog biscuits and pieces of baloney and then stretch out on their living room rug, sighing with happy satisfaction. He had it made and I thought, "Good for him." He had people who loved and cared for him, a stable home with us, regular meals, and lots of hugs and kisses.

14

Spring was here, and it was time to reconnect with all that had been buried during the lengthy winter months. The warmer temperatures and longer days brought more daylight; I was like a new flower, lifting every petal toward the sun. I despise the cold and could feel my energy returning after a long hibernation. The dogs (and me) were overdue for some regular, lengthy walks. In the winter, it was a quick trip out to do their business and then, except for Eddie and his own set of rules, we went quickly back inside. Now with the air turning, we were getting back outside on a regular basis. The solar panels in my brain were being recharged.

As the weather improved, we would often take a short car ride to Ravenswood Park in Gloucester. This deeply wooded nature reserve has ten miles of carriage paths and lots of interesting, twisty trails. The dogs always enjoyed the car ride—heads and tongues hanging out of the back windows, spit and drool streaking the car doors. Other dogs and their owners also flooded the park, eager for all the new smells and change of scenery.

It was like a reunion of long-lost friends, the humans hugging and chatting and, naturally, the dogs sniffing each other's butts. Both Wolfie and Eddie spent most of their time outside now, watched over by Steve. It was an unspoken agreement. He loved both dogs, but we knew Eddie was his favorite and the bond between them was evident.

"There you are, Eddie boy!" Steve would exclaim. "How's my boy today?" He rustled the furry hair on his head like Eddie was a youngster. Eddie would push up against him, intimate in a way that he wasn't with anyone else. We officially dubbed Steve Eddie's grandfather, and Steve seemed to enjoy this endearing title. Steve was always warm and loving toward Eddie. It was touching and adorable to witness. They seemed to be kindred spirits, bound together from another lifetime.

One day a friend of Steve's son had stopped by to drop something off at his home. Eddie had settled himself behind the friend's truck, lounging in Steve's driveway, the pavement warm from the sun. As he was leaving, the driver did not notice that Eddie had taken up residence behind his truck. Eddie, completely oblivious and sleeping soundly, didn't cry out until the truck had run over his back legs and tail. The driver had not only backed over him, but when he realized what he had done, he also lurched forward, further crushing Eddie's tail and damaging the skin on both of his back legs.

Fortunately, I was home and heard the commotion coming from Steve's yard. I raced out my back door and found Eddie bleeding and panting heavily in the middle of Steve's driveway. He looked like he had a terrible case of road rash with abrasions all over his back legs. There wasn't any blood on his tail, so I didn't believe that it had been injured. Steve stayed with Eddie while I ran for my truck. *Here we go again?* I managed to stay calm despite knowing that he was injured— it didn't seem too serious in that moment. My medical training as an x-ray technologist helped me to focus on him without panicking.

By the time I returned with the truck, Steve had wrapped some old dishcloths around Eddie's bleeding legs and now his tail, as well. The skin on his back feet had been torn away and looked very sore. I phoned our new vet, Donna, before leaving my house so she would be ready for him with an injection of pain medication. We wanted Eddie to be comfortable and sleepy enough for the staff to take some x-rays of his lacerations.

"Oh, Eddie boy! Oh, Eddie boy!" Steve was near tears, standing helplessly in the driveway. We carefully loaded Eddie into the backseat of my truck and off we went to the veterinary office—again. I promised to call Steve with an update as I floored my truck out of his driveway. *Eddie, why do these distressing events keep happening to you??*

The injuries didn't look too bad on the outside, but the tests showed the reality of the situation: disastrous trauma had been done. The bushiness of his fur had hidden the injuries underneath—Eddie's tail had been crushed directly in the middle, damaging not only the bones in his tail but the nerve endings, too. In less than a year, our "free dog" was jacking up my credit card balance and driving my blood pressure into the stratosphere. In the short eight months that we'd had Eddie, this was round three on the merry-go-round of veterinary visits. I was weary from the adrenaline-filled ride but worried about him, nonetheless.

15

Vet Donna splinted and wrapped Eddie's tail and wrapped his back feet, informing us that the healing process would be extensive. Eddie would have to be kept inside, except for bathroom breaks. This scenario was starting to sound familiar. Eddie was clearly in pain, and we kept him as comfortable as possible while he convalesced at home on stacks of soft, plush comforters. We were going to have to spend weeks bringing his food and water to him, keeping him pain-free on a steady dose of doggie dope.

For the first week, we had to carry him outside to do his business because his feet were so sore and heavily bandaged. He weighed fifty pounds, so this wasn't easy. Steve felt terrible, as if the accident was his fault. He visited often in those weeks of confinement, usually with a Milk Bone or two and a few slices of American cheese.

Eddie looked persistently glum, his eyes sad and downcast, his doggy grin replaced by a dull panting. As a result of the trauma, his tail wouldn't wag, leaving us to guess whether he was happy to see us or even happy at all. A dog's tail is a communication tool, and Eddie's was broken. His tail hung off of his butt like a wet wig, wrapped in blue and white hospital tape. His feet were bandaged up the same way—they looked like furry hockey sticks. Once again, our hapless adopted son was down for most of that month. Wolfie would sometimes squeeze herself onto the blankets with him, licking his face and sniffing gently at his wounds.

I envisioned Wolfie thinking, *"Dude, what the hell....more boo-boo's?"* But she'd snuggle with him in his sick bed, soothing him, head on his back or front paws. I'm sure he was jealous of her ability to run around while he was bedridden. He could only lie there, lethargic on Rimadyl (the doggie version of Ibuprofen) and watch as life went on as if he were in jail—again.

A month of nonstop bandage changes and repeated x-rays determined that the bones were starting to remedy but the nerve damage to his tail could be permanent. Eddie was on antibiotics to stave off any infections to his wounds and his feet were healing, but his tail remained paralyzed.

Vet Donna tried desperately to save Eddie's tail, but after two months, it was not mending properly and still hung dormant off of his back end. He chewed at it constantly. We agreed with Donna's recommendation to amputate the infected tail with the hope that it would heal over time. Donna wanted to keep Eddie overnight in preparation for his surgery, so we brought in his favorite blanket, loved him up, and left until morning. Eddie, however, had other plans—that little schemer's tail may not have been swishing, but his gray matter launched into what I now refer to as "Operation Wild Dog Instinct."

16

After we had arrived home, had dinner, and settled in for a movie, the phone rang. It was around 8:00 p.m., and the caller ID showed the vet's office number. *Uh-oh.* Vet Donna was on the phone. She sounded tentative and a little upset, her voice an octave higher than usual.

"Eddie is okay," she spit out quickly, "but there is a problem." "What's wrong, Donna? Should we come down to the office?" I held my breath, raising my eyebrows to alert the rest of the family that some potentially bad news was coming.

"In all of my years as a veterinarian, I have never seen this happen before, and I've only read about it while training in college." Donna's voice was on edge. She seemed to be vacillating with each sentence. *What in the world was she talking about?* A light sweat broke out on my upper lip. "I went back into the surgery area to check on Eddie once more before I left for the night, and, well, I am just so sorry. I have never, ever seen this before." She sounded so bewildered and nervous that my breath started to falter and catch. "Donna, just tell me. Did Eddie die? What happened? Please just tell me!" I swallowed a few times because my voice sounded small and dry.

"When I went back to check on Eddie...he had torn away all of the bandaging...and had chewed off his infected tail."

There it was. I didn't know how to react. I was stunned. Both Frank and Samantha were poking me, begging for information. I held my finger up to have them wait a moment.

"Does this mean that he won't need surgery or that his life is in danger?" She was taking so long to answer each question, pondering what to tell me.

"In the morning I will have to put him under anesthesia, surgically clean up the wound, and attend to it to ensure its healing, but he is not in any danger."

"Eddie's okay, you guys," I said. "I'll tell you the rest in a minute." My head started to pound as I wondered how I was going to explain to them what had happened.

My mind was racing, visualizing Eddie gnawing off his own tail, the blood and the smell of infection driving him mad in such a primal way. It was also rather intriguing—and gross. I could picture the bloody stump at the bottom of the cage and Eddie's triumphant face, proud of his own surgical skills. He was probably relieved that it was over.

"I just can't tell you enough how sorry I am that this has happened," Donna continued. "I really can't believe it. Animals in the wild are known to do this when they have injuries to their limbs either from traps or fights with other animals. If they can smell that their limb is 'dead,' they will actually remove it themselves. I've just never seen a pet do it."

Well, Eddie was not an ordinary pet now, was he?!

"Donna, please don't worry about it." I was certain that she was concerned that we would be angry or maybe sue her for damages, so I reassured her. "I am just relieved that it happened when he was with you in a controlled environment and that it can be tended to right away. Where do we go from here?"

Donna told me that Eddie would be given some medicine to help him sleep. She surmised that the nerve endings in his tail were presumably dead since he didn't seem to be in any pain. This did nothing to assuage my agitation and worry, but at this point, what could I do?

Vet Donna and her astonished team had Eddie on the operating table first thing in the morning. They cleaned up the hack job he had done on his tail and re-bandaged it for the next round of healing. The remaining tail still looked dead, and even though there was a small chance that it could wag again, we weren't all that hopeful. Eddie's tail was now a swollen, fat little nub, half the size of a plump, overcooked hot dog. He had just added another unbelievable story to his repertoire of adventures. He was setting precedence for hobo dogs everywhere.

The upside to this mishap was the reaction of the veterinary staff. Eddie was a bit of a mythological figure come to life, a college textbook story in the flesh. He was an official doggie celebrity, a reality television star in the making. The duration of time that we'd had with Eddie was colored with many firsts for us as pet owners, and his destiny with the weird and extraordinary didn't end there. If we only could have capitalized on that reality show concept...

17

Over the next several months, Eddie's stump began to heal. He looked like he was wearing a tail turban, wrapped up in various colors of medical tape. Each time we took him for his biweekly vet visits, his little tail was a tiny bit less swollen. It looked like a hairless ding-dong because it had been shaved. It still didn't wag, and we resigned ourselves to the fact that it probably wasn't ever going to wag again. I secretly held out hope.

I felt bad for Eddie—it was like his smile had been erased from his face. Imagine not being able to smile anymore. It may have bothered me more than it bothered him, I don't know. Without an enthusiastic tail wag, he didn't appear to be excited to see us when we came home from work or school. He still greeted us at the door to give stinky kisses (his breath was still a challenge to keep fresh) and turn his backside for some good scratching. After that, he wanted out.

During his healing time, we limited his roaming abilities to after work hours. He and Wolfie would head out together after a day indoors, happy for the fresh air and the chance to check out what the neighborhood dogs had been up to; butt sniffing was like a call to duty. I would watch the two of them from the window and think, *I wonder what the other dogs think of his tail? Is he having "Rudolph the Red-Nosed Reindeer" moments where the other dogs are frightened of his deformity?*

They certainly didn't mind sniffing it. I think they were curious, especially since he couldn't "wave" to them anymore. Maybe they thought he was a snob, with his nub tail, immovable and floppy. I just hoped that he wasn't being bullied or being given the silent treatment because of his lack of tail interaction. I kept my eyes on him, like a momma bear, ready to rescue her cub.

After many months, the hair on Eddie's tail started to grow back and the bandages were removed for good. He looked a little silly, this beautiful, fluffy shepherd/husky-mix boy with his abbreviated little hot dog tail, disabled and silent. But his spirits were back to normal, his days once again his own and his love affair with Steve not missing a beat. He went over to Steve's house each morning after gallivanting in the neighborhood.

One day Frank and I were with Eddie and Wolfie, chatting in Steve's driveway, enjoying a late-summer evening. We were telling Steve the uncomfortable news that we were building a house in Gloucester and would soon be moving away. We had been avoiding this chat for months.

"It's in a wooded area without any traffic. Eddie and Wolfie will be safer when they are outdoors." I was trying to convince Steve into thinking that this was a good idea. Steve was silent, smiling politely while we were selling him on our plan.

"We're going to have a nice lawn, too. Eddie can enjoy lying in the nice soft, green grass." Frank was trying hard to make it sound great. Steve kept grinning and nodding, but he couldn't hide the sadness in his eyes.

"We'll only be about five miles from here, Steve. We can bring Eddie back for visits any time you want! We may even need you to doggie-sit him for us occasionally. Would you be interested in doing that for us?" I was trying to reassure Steve that he would see Eddie again. At that moment, Steve reached down to pat Eddie's head.

"My Eddie boy, you better come and visit me now. Who will help me around the yard?" The tight sound of Steve's voice made me feel like crying. I was looking away from the two of them, tilting my neck back, trying to roll the teardrops back into my eyes.

And then it happened.

It started slowly with only a flicker of movement. I placed my hand on Frank's shoulder and quietly said, "Look, look!" I kept my voice low and steady, not wanting the miracle to turn into a mirage. But it was real: Eddie's tail was moving—moving like the limbs of a paralyzed man, rusty and stiff but moving. Steve knelt next to him, astonished.

"Eddie, Eddie, my Eddie boy! Are you happy to see me?" Steve was almost breathless. His face was smiling like Eddie had just come back from the dead. Eddie's tail was lifted ever so slightly, doing a back-and-forth slow dance (like "twerking" but in the '90s). We all laughed out loud, and as we hugged each other, the wagging became a little stronger, a little more pronounced. Wolfie began to stiff Eddie's tail. Even she seemed surprised.

"I'm so happy to see your tail wagging again!" I felt warm with relief and gratitude. I couldn't wait to call our vet and tell her the news. I felt that Steve was instrumental in Eddie's "will to wag." He loved Steve so much that he had probably been working on using his tail again during his recovery. We lobbed silly theories back and forth:

"Maybe he's been going to doggie physical therapy behind our backs?"

"Maybe he's been doing doggie yoga in secret with Wolfie?"

"Maybe he's been watching *How to Get Your Wag Back* on Animal Planet?"

Or maybe, it was simply a real miracle. Each day the wagging became stronger, even though it did look a tad hilarious. Eddie's tail nub was a sight to behold. Eddie could "smile" again, and we were all incredibly grateful. We couldn't wait to show the neighborhood dogs.

18

Once again, Eddie was the star of the veterinary office. We brought him in so he could show off his new wagging abilities. There were squeals of delight from the staff, and Vet Donna was eager to see for herself what Eddie's tail was thought to never do again.

"Well, Eddie, you haven't failed to impress me yet." A camera came out, and the picture taking began. This miracle had to be documented for all to see; it was a phenomenon. Even though Eddie was looking at Donna with happy eyes and panting into her face, I could see that he was not comfortable being there. His eyes zoomed around when Donna wasn't looking, nose smelling the air, no doubt reliving some memories. It felt like exposure therapy in what Eddie may have deemed "the office building of bad luck."

It was nice to see him fawned over, but I kept the visit short and hustled him back into the truck, where Wolfie was waiting. We didn't want to go back there for a long time. He wasn't a carnival sideshow attraction to be gawked over, like the bearded lady. He slumped next to Wolfie in the back, exhausted from his showing. I took them both for ice cream to thank Eddie for his performance. I prayed that our next visit to the vet's office would be for a regular checkup. We were all due for a break from veterinary drama. But wait—did I say something about bad luck?

19

It was now deep into the fall of 1997, with darkness enveloping our city by 3:45 p.m. Turning back the clock in New England is hated by many. I detest this time of year—the dark, the colder days and nights, the (gasp!) holidays. Ugh. It was akin to impending doom.

School was in full swing again for Sam, so we hit the ground running each day. We also schlepped back and forth between our rental home in Rockport, work, school, and the new house in the midst of being built in Gloucester. There were so many decisions to make, so many construction projects to manage. Some may call these "luxury problems," but it was stressful for all of us, as the date was getting closer for the move—and taking Eddie from Steve.

I was also worried about the change for our dogs. They didn't have a say in the move and even though it would be safer for them and off the busy street we lived on, Wolfie and Eddie were happy where they were. This was where their friends and family lived, and I'm sure that they didn't see any reason to leave. I felt guilty. This was a "trying to save our marriage" house, and I was worried that it wasn't going to work. Dogs are blissfully unaware of break-ups and long-range plans for the future. Dogs live in the moment. I still strive for this every day.

Frank and I hadn't been happy for quite a while, and though we weren't yelling and screaming at each other, there was a total disconnect. Going through the motions was our daily routine. We were good people in a not-so-great union, and we were trying our best to make it last. I had hopes that the geographical cure of a new home would be our best chance. It certainly gave us other things to focus on besides each other.

Each night, I would let the dogs out for one last hurrah before bedtime. Once it became dark by four o'clock, I usually went out with them. We were in a nice suburban neighborhood, but there were still cars that occasionally went about twenty-five miles per hour past our house.

One night, I was home alone and felt like I was coming down with the flu. I didn't want to go outside with the dogs, preferring to stay in bed, where I had spent most of the day. No one else was home, so I let the dogs out and returned to my bed, knowing that I would get up in fifteen or twenty minutes to call them back inside. They were both good like that, coming when I called them. This night was different from the rest, though. I dozed off, buzzed on cold medicine, my limbs feeling listless and weak. A screech of brakes woke me from my stupor. I was a little confused, as if I had awakened from a long slumber. I went down to the door and called outside to the dogs.

"Wolfie! Eddie! Time to come in now! Come on, kids, let's go!" I shivered on the steps, waiting for them to appear. Eddie trotted around the corner without Wolfie but didn't come onto the porch. He was standing at the bottom step as if he were in shock, silent and still.

"Come in, Eddie. Where's Wolfie?" Eddie stood somberly for a moment then took off toward the back of the house and Steve's property. It was in this moment that I remembered the screech of car tires. *No, no, no, no, no! Not my girl!*

I went back inside and was pulling on a coat when the phone rang. I grabbed it and started to tell whomever it was that I'd call them back. I stopped short when an unfamiliar voice said, "Ms. Dexter? Do you own a black and white dog? This is Officer Lesch."

I knew in that moment that Wolfie was gone. I started to babble, asking where he was, where my dog was. He told me that he was in front of Steve's house, in the street. I started to shake, feeling grief begin to shatter my heart, one piece at a time. I struggled through the dark backyard, slipping on the frosted dew on the lawn in my L.L.

Bean slippers and no socks. I could see the blue flashing lights from the police vehicle. My heart took a long, frightening dive.

Eddie slowly stepped around the officer to meet me like an undertaker at a funeral. I instantly became hysterical on the inside, appearing quieter and more shocked on the outside.

As I write this today, my body clearly and painfully remembers the feeling of grief, sadness, and guilt. I am experiencing fresh tears and my fingers go cold while writing it down. My heart felt like it had stopped beating, but at the same time was sick with heartache. The officer had picked Wolfie up from the ground and placed her in the trunk of his patrol car, not knowing if he would be able to reach me or not.

"I spoke to the driver. He was distraught." The officer softly held onto my shoulder as he spoke. "He said that there was a group of dogs crossing the street in front of him, and he slowed to let them by. As he accelerated again, a few more ran out from the yard and one of them hit her head on his back tailgate." Even Officer Lesch had tears in his eyes. Wolfie's neck had been snapped by the force and she died instantly. She was ten years old.

Wolfie was my first real dog, not my parents' dog, but my dog, my responsibility. I had rescued her as an abandoned puppy when I lived in California with Sam for one short year in 1988. Back then, she was covered in fleas and scared to death of everything. But Sam and I had brought her along when we returned to Massachusetts. She was ours, our funny little girl-dog, Wolfie. Wolfgang Amadeus Mozart. *Sam. How was I going to tell Sam?*

I asked the officer if he would drive around to my house and carry her in for me. Eddie and I walked back through the yard. Every time I looked at Eddie, I burst into fresh tears. He had lost his best buddy, and I felt completely responsible. I am not sure where Steve was, for my memory of that time is solely focused on Wolfie and those events. If he came out of his house, I don't remember it. I think he did. I just don't know.

Officer Lesch was so kind and gentle. He lifted Wolfie out of the trunk and carried her into the house. I didn't know what to do. I asked him to carry her down into the basement where it was cooler, and he lay her on a table off of the floor.

I covered her with a blanket as if to warm her. I wasn't going to take her body anywhere tonight. I thanked and hugged the officer as he left us in our kitchen, my emotions shot to pieces, my body numb and on fire at the same time. I returned to the basement with Eddie, crying hysterically while hugging Wolfie's lifeless body.

My phone was ringing upstairs, but it was just a blur of sound in the background. I was flush with tears and sorrow. I couldn't fathom letting go of Wolfie. The ringing wouldn't stop, so I reluctantly left her side to answer it. On the other end of the line was the man who had hit and killed Wolfie. Jay. I didn't know him, but he lived just up the street. He was crying and apologizing, telling me how much he loved dogs and had never hit one in his whole life. I found myself deeply touched by his angst, and I knew then that it had been a horrible accident. I forgave him, for what was I to do? I had let Wolfie and Eddie outside in the dark. It was my fault. I couldn't be angry or blame the driver. I was incredibly despondent, my chest buckling with the weight of the pain.

• Jay • -j: of Hooper Court reported last night about 6:30 that he had hit
a dog while driving up High Street.
The dog, owned by Stacy G. of 5
Parker St., died at the scene.

20

Telling Sam and Frank what happened to Wolfie was a nightmare I would rather forget. I had to tell Frank over the phone, and it was the first time I had ever heard him cry out in pain. Sam wept as much as I did, but she barricaded her teen-aged self in her room, brokenhearted in her grief. I didn't sleep for three days and couldn't go to work. My incredibly generous workplace gave me three days of bereavement pay. It was as if a family member had died. It felt exactly the same. Any dog lover will attest to this feeling of losing a pet to losing a member of your family. The accident played before me like a horror movie, one I was forced to watch, over and over, as I paced around at night. I tortured myself with painful feelings of blame and regret. It was crushing.

I could continue to supplement this story with details of those weeks following Wolfie's untimely demise, but I just don't have it in me to keep reliving it. I can share with you that Eddie was like a ghost. He wandered the house, sniffing Wolfie's blanket, combing the neighborhood for any signs of her. I felt guilty just looking at his sad face. I knew that he was missing Wolfie just as much as we were; he would whine for no reason and didn't eat much the first few weeks that she was gone. Before her death, he would sleep downstairs. Now he was coming upstairs to sleep in our bedroom. He'd circle himself into a nest of blankets next to our bed, seeming to long for our company and our comfort. I cried many nights into his neck, grateful for his presence and his loving furry face. Eddie was showing a vulnerability that I hadn't seen in him before; he was always the tough hobo dog, bothered by nothing. We were all devastated.

I tried getting back to my routine, staying busy to shove away the torturous thoughts of the way Wolfie's life had ended. It truly felt as if I would never get over her loss. I dreamed of her. I couldn't bring myself to remove her bowl from the floor.

I knew that someday I would have to bring another female dog into my life. Since adding Eddie into our family, I had started to believe that life was better with two dogs, a boy and a girl. *Maybe after we move. Maybe adopt a greyhound.* This was something that I had always wanted to do, and maybe the time was right. But not just yet, for it was much too soon.

R.I.P. Wolfie

21

Before Wolfie's death, I had been taking both dogs to the new house in Gloucester a few times a week to let them get used to the area, letting them sniff the "new" air and the woods beside the property. My heart was soggy with fresh tears, knowing that Wolfie was never going to get to experience it with us. But I kept taking Eddie because we were still moving, still pretending that everything was going to be okay.

This tragedy was another distraction from the troubled relationship between me and Frank, and we plowed into our new normal with fresh wounds. Several times a week, Eddie and I now had our own field trip to the new place for a walk around the property. We would walk round and round the unfinished foundation, me usually in a daze, Eddie forming his own opinions.

Each week more walls were built, paint colors chosen, and arrange-ments made for the big move. It was the summer of 1998, and it was time for Eddie and Steve to say goodbye to their daily routine. I assured Steve that I would be bringing Eddie back for visits. *How is Eddie going to get along without Steve and vice-versa?* However, I was to be baffled once again; Eddie would devise a plan to get what he wanted, and we would be bewildered by his intelligence. Truly. He wasn't going to give up his beloved routine. Not a chance.

22

After the move, I decided to take a week off to organize our belongings and adjust to our new space. I wasn't ready to let Eddie outside every day without some guidance, so I planned to be around as he adjusted, too. It was June and the weather was warm, but not too hot, the woods smelling of new growth and possibilities. Eddie was able to be outside all day while I unpacked, arranged furniture, and contemplated my new life as a homeowner. Eddie seemed to be adapting perfectly to the woods, and I breathed a sigh of relief, seeing his happy grin returning a little each day.

When the day came for me to finally return to work, I said a little prayer while I let Eddie out for his first day alone. *Please God, watch over my Eddie today.* He trotted off into the woods with nary a glance behind him. There were no cars traveling back and forth. We had built our home in a new and mostly undeveloped area, and the road was still full of ruts and potholes. No one would be traveling into the neighborhood unless they lived there, and we didn't have any neighbors yet. He was fine. I drove out of the driveway, not realizing that I was holding my breath until I reached the end of the jarring and uneven dirt road.

Returning home after 5:00 p.m., I noticed that Frank had gotten home before me.

"Seen Eddie?" Frank had not seen Eddie. "Did you call him?" Multiple times.

Just then, the house phone rang. It was Steve's number on the caller ID. I didn't dare tell him that Eddie's first day of freedom had resulted in a disappearance. "Hey there, Steve. How are you?" I tried to sound normal, hoping he wouldn't hear the uncertainty in my voice. "Oh, I'm great, Stacey! How's the new house?" Banal chitchat. "Fine, Steve, just fine. What's up?" I was hoping that he was calling to invite Eddie over for a playdate later in the week.

"Did you drop Eddie off in Rockport today?" *Huh?* "What are you talking about, Steve?" *Of course, we didn't drop him off in Rockport!* "What do you mean?" *What in the world had Eddie been up to now??*

"Well, Eddie showed up late this morning, like he always used to, so I figured that you must have driven him into town. He's here, at my house."

Okay, what?? How had Eddie gotten to Rockport, over five miles from our new home? We certainly had never walked him from one town to the other. And unless dogs could figure out the route like a doggie GPS, how was this even possible?

"Steve, I swear to you, no one gave Eddie a ride to Rockport. I let him out this morning before leaving for work. I was home for the first week at the new house, letting him out every day. He always came back when we called him."

"Huh," Steve replied. "Then I wonder how he got here?" *Good question!* I could picture Steve scratching the top of his head while looking at Eddie. "It's another Eddie mystery, I guess. Thanks for calling. I'll be right over."

Well, this was a new one. A dog that could walk back to his favorite place? How had he gotten himself to Steve's? I figured that this was a one-time thing, a fluke. But Eddie had his mind, and his route, made up.

For the next few weeks when we returned home at the end of the workday, we would call for Eddie, he would not appear, we would call Steve, and he'd be in Rockport! It got to the point that Steve said that each time we would call, right around five o'clock, Eddie would automatically go to the front door and wait for one of us to come and get him. Now I'm picking up my dog? He had us trained! Which one of us belonged to Pavlov?

We had no idea how he was getting to Steve's. There were miles of dense, unbuildable woods between our new neighborhood and the town of Rockport. We could only surmise that Eddie was using his sense of smell and his instincts to get himself from our house in Gloucester to Rockport, to continue his daily routine with Steve. It was amazing.

When we were home on the weekends, he would stay around. The traveling phenomenon only happened during the week. Eddie proved to us that even though my dad called him "the Brick," he was far from stupid. He was not going to give up his established daily routine *or* Steve. We often fantasized about attaching a device to his head, an "Eddie Cam," to track his movements and find out just how he was getting to Steve's house. We had a theory of a possible route through the woods, but no real proof. This was long before the invention of the Go-Pro camera, which we would've loved to have back then.

Eddie was an enigma. I only hoped that he remained safe on his journeys back and forth through the woods. His hobo street smarts seemed to make him fearless. I knew that locking him up all day or tying him on a lead outside would be cruel for a dog like Eddie. I feared if we took such action that he would eventually flee from us, too, like he had from the other owners that had tried to tame him the past. We had to accept Eddie for the way he was or more than likely he would say, "Adios, amigos!"

23

That summer was uneventful though I was dreaming of having a girl dog again. I had always wanted to adopt a greyhound, an ex-racer from the dog tracks. I had seen a horrific documentary about the lives of these precious creatures and the dire need for adopted "forever" homes. The dog racing industry was merciless in the way it treated dogs that were no longer winning or injured. They would be euthanized in large groups and callously thrown away. To me, this was criminal, and thankfully, in 2010, dog racing was banned in Massachusetts.

I started to research local greyhound shelters and found one about an hour and a half from our home. Frank wasn't into it, but Sam and I were, so one day we all made the drive up to the shelter and chose a sweet, female greyhound named Ida Mae. She was all black, except for her white feet, a white streak down the middle of her face, and a white tip on her tail.

Her name should have been the overused cliché of Nervous Nellie; she shook like an aftershock of an earthquake and seemed frightened by the most ordinary sounds. I couldn't imagine her racing. I have no idea how she survived the sound of the starting gun. She looked remarkably similar to Wolfie, though she was by far more skittish. We paid the $150, received a few specific greyhound tips from the woman at the kennel, then carefully placed her into the back seat with Sam. Frank had to lift her in because we couldn't get her to jump. We were also told that greyhounds had to be taught how to navigate stairs. Their lives as a commodity did not expose them to pet-like experiences of a real home. All they knew were kennels and racing. Ida Mae had been treated like a "thing."

We were told that she had been shipped up from a Florida racetrack in a large truck with other greyhounds who were also deemed losers. She had raced maybe fourteen times, and since she wasn't a winner, goodbye! Before greyhound rescue shelters became available, the dogs were euthanized. All business. It was a distressing thought. I wanted to save them all.

We had a cozy blanket for her first ride in our car. Sam was a calming presence for her, patting and speaking lovingly to her all the way home. Ida Mae's first treat was a couple bites of hamburger and a few French fries from a McDonald's drive-thru. Our new girl seemed to like fast food a *lot*. She looked so cute, gently nibbling on her bits and pieces, even drinking a little water from a small bowl that we had brought with us. She was like a dainty Southern belle, manners, and all.

We had high hopes that she could fit right in at home and felt that Eddie would be happy to have a new female buddy. He was so easy-going and non-aggressive. I was sure that he would gladly show her the ropes, or at least his version of the ropes, of being a family pet. Eddie had a thing or two to learn when we took him off the streets, but with his guide Wolfie by his side, they had worked out an arrangement that worked for everybody. Now Eddie would be the teacher. It was going to be interesting to see just what he would be "teaching" his new student.

Ida Mae with Eddie

24

It was late November when we brought Ida Mae home to meet Eddie. We had lived at our new place for about six months, and Eddie had the lay of the land in the neighborhood. He wasn't going off to Rockport nearly as much, so we felt that he would be a good guide for his new sister, not leading her down some unknown path across two towns. We thought about changing her name, like we had with Eddie. We went through various clichéd names for a black and white dog, including "Oreo," "Blackie," and "Midnight," none of which seemed to fit her. Since she was our own Southern belle, over the next few days, I gave her a Southern-accented "voice," speaking her needs or thoughts, and the name Ida Mae just stuck. I could hear her voice, like Scarlett O'Hara's, admonishing Eddie: "Now Eddie, you have GOT to get that flatulence under control."

Eddie took to her like they had been friends their whole lives. There was no rivalry between them. Day after day, Eddie kept up his usual routine with Ida Mae trotting close behind, learning the ropes. He taught her how to go up and down the stairs in the house, where the chow and the water bowls were, and the good spots to "go" outside. She was a quick study.

In the greyhound racing industry, these dogs are born and bred for racing. They spend most of their time in kennels on a concrete floor. They don't live in a home until they are "retired," when they are deemed too slow, age out, or have been injured. Once a greyhound breaks a limb, they are through racing. No one ever puts any money into fixing their broken bones, as the owners know that they will never be as fast as they once were ever again. The damaged ones are taken in by the greyhound rescues, bones healed, senses soothed, and then adopted out to loving homes.

Ida Mae *loved* the softness of a couch or lounging on her cushy comforter. She would stretch out in the patches of warm sun that would shine through the windows and sigh blissfully, her body comfortable on the plush carpet or microfiber ottoman. She was settling in, and we were all getting to know one another. It was during this time that we started to notice the list of things that she was afraid of.

The trash truck came on Thursdays, and the sound of that truck was one of her biggest fears. She could hear it coming long before she could see it. She would start to pace around the house, looking frantic and jumpy. The first time it happened, I figured that she had never heard one before, so it was a new, scary sound. Eddie, of course, was oblivious. He did not scare easily, so the two of them were true opposites. After a few weeks, I assumed that this reaction would go away. However, her face would be full of alarm each time *any* truck came into the neighborhood.

One trash day I couldn't find her; she had gone upstairs and hidden in the shower stall, shaking and cowering. It was pathetic the way the grunting, grinding, and banging of the truck could cause her so much fear. She would shake all over. We had a theory about the "truck terrors." She had been shipped up in a large truck with many other greyhounds, usually ten to twenty at a time. It must have been terrifying for her. How would we ever make her feel safe?

Ida Mae Fee-Fee

25

Outside, the trees were bare, the wind shoving the crispy brown leaves around the yard. Ida did not care for those sounds, either. When we went out to walk in the morning (Eddie still stayed outside most days, but I walked them in the morning), she would stare up at the menacing, scraping branches, hear the crinkling of the leaves, and trot faster and faster, like she was trying to outrun the sounds. We soon discovered that she also hated flying things like kites on the beach, balloons, airplanes, and even an errant plastic grocery bag, blowing down the street. It was as if she felt that these things would somehow attack her.

In the very beginning, she was a nightmare to walk on a leash, always looking petrified and wanting to bolt. She would stop and stand like a statue, frozen in place. Nothing would move her until she wanted to move. Eddie didn't care or notice any of these things. He would just stand in the road, waiting for a bit, while I pleaded with Ida Mae to keep walking. We didn't have to leash Eddie, and eventually he would go on ahead on one of his missions.

Greyhounds are sight hounds, their eyesight sharper than most dogs. We felt that this attributed to her fears, her eyesight a detriment, seeing everything, good or bad. Our theory seemed to ring true because at night when we would walk, it was if the dark tamped down all the sights, cloaking them in the blackness, and she was much calmer and less afraid. At night, she couldn't readily see all the scary things. Nighttime was Ida time.

26

We'd had Ida Mae for about a month when the Christmas season was upon us once again. Ida Mae was fascinated by the pine tree inside the house and was curious about the pretty hanging decorations, the twinkling of little bells and lights, the glitter reflecting in her eyes. I had taken some time off to acclimate her and felt confident that she would be okay with Eddie while I was at work. It was becoming much colder now, and we kept Eddie inside. I needed him to keep an eye on Ida. When I left the two of them, I reminded Eddie that he was in charge, raising my eyebrows at him while he flopped onto his side. As I left that first morning, they were each on their beds, looking warm and cozy.

Later, upon my return, I opened the door quietly, trying to see if I could spy on them, see what they might be up to, like they were teenagers left alone for the first time. I had the door open a crack when Ida appeared, holding a little plastic Santa Claus ornament between her teeth. She scampered off when she saw me. I had to laugh at how mischievous her face looked, holding Santa in her lips, a little "o." "What have you got there, girl?" I teased. I caught a glimpse of Eddie and congratulated him on his babysitting prowess. "Thanks a lot, Eddie." He seemed to shrug as if to say, "Whatever, she's alive."

As I went further into the house, I saw the Christmas tree lying on the living room floor. It looked like it had been knocked around a bit, its ornaments used as dog toys. I peered over at Eddie. He had started to pant and was looking at the door, as if it was his time to escape.

"I'm innocent!" he seemed to say. "It was all her!"

Ida still had Santa in her mouth, his head peeking out from between her little front teeth. How could I be angry? I just laughed and started to chase her around the house, trying to get Santa back. Ida was having fun, and I was enjoying her gleefulness.

I eventually rescued Santa, righted the tree, and replaced the scattered ornaments. Eddie remained standing at the front door––*ahem*––ready to go out, babysitting duties over.

It was the first time that I had seen Ida Mae truly relaxed and feeling safe. It was what I had been praying for; I really wanted her to feel that she was home, that this *was* her home. We took it day by day, for it was going to take a lot longer than we had originally thought. The gleeful moments were fleeting.

27

The first few weeks after we had Ida Mae, I wasn't sure that we would be keeping her. There were times that she seemed like she was finally settling in, walking a bit better on leash, making new friends on the morning walks. However, she was still forever hiding from sounds near and far, terrified by so many normal things. One day, I was on the phone with the greyhound rescue in Mendon, voicing my concerns about her behavior and asking for advice. I was on a landline phone with a long, curly cord.

As I was going over some options with the kennel worker, Ida Mae walked by me, got spooked by I don't know what, got her dog tags caught in the phone cord, freaked out, and bolted away like a cartoon character, eyes bulging. She dragged the phone and answering machine off the kitchen counter with her, crashing and banging down the hallway into the den. The woman at the rescue kennel heard the commotion, listening to me as I tossed the receiver down to unravel a shaking and panicked Ida Mae from all the cords while trying to calm her down and put everything back.

I was out of breath when I returned to the phone. "This is what I'm talking about! She overreacts to everything!" I was exasperated. Between the trash trucks, blowing branches, flying things, and any loud noise, she was miserable and my nerves were shot. *Were we the right forever home?* I was starting to doubt it.

Eddie usually just ignored her, watching her reactions but never reacting himself. He didn't get it, either. She also wouldn't walk more than one hundred feet from the house before stopping in her tracks, freezing like a statue, and looking up the road, petrified. She would literally stop walking, randomly, and not budge. I tried pulling and pushing, eventually sometimes picking her up and carrying her back home.

We would walk both dogs early in the morning in this beautiful wooded reservoir, hoping that it was quiet enough for Ida to feel safe. Eddie would go on ahead, using his nose as a compass. Unfortunately, each time another person would approach or a jogger would run up the trail, Ida would back up into the forest as far as her leash would allow until they passed us. This behavior was getting old.

The woman at the kennel was sympathetic but didn't have much advice beyond giving her more time. She offered to take her back to try and re-home her if we were sure that she wasn't a good fit. I hung up feeling defeated, my hand resting a while on the receiver. I *was* sympathetic, but I felt my patience growing thin. I wondered if she'd ever get comfortable in everyday life.

In desperation, we called a dog trainer to see if he could help her. Her anxiety was so high, I felt she may need to be medicated. He helped for the hour that he was at the house, but after that, there was no change. Eddie watched from the dining room during Ida's session like he was taking notes. *He* didn't need a therapist and he was an orphan. In those moments, Eddie really must've been missing Wolfie.

28

One night about three weeks into Ida Mae's adoption, I had another conversation with the folks at the greyhound rescue kennel. We replayed our previous conversation from the phone cord debacle. What would returning her to the rescue mean for her? I felt incredibly guilty. I hung up the phone without deciding what to do. I was upstairs, sitting on the floor of my bedroom, leaning against the bed. I let out the breath I was holding, closed my eyes, and asked for a sign. *Please God, please give me a sign. Should we keep Ida Mae?*

As I opened my eyes, there stood Ida in the doorway. I gave her a guilty half smile, hoping she hadn't heard my plea. We locked eyes, and as Ida Mae walked into the room toward me and got closer, she lowered her head so that when she reached me, she pushed the top of her little greyhound head against my heart. She stood there quiet and calm. I had received my sign.

My arms embraced her warm chest, and I covered her nose with kisses, thanking God for the guidance. I pledged to Ida, "You are in your forever home. I will never send you back to the shelter, no matter what." I called the rescue people back, told the woman what happened, and never called her again. Best. Story. Ever.

I called out to Eddie, "Hey, Ed! Ida Mae's staying, just in case you were wondering!" I went downstairs and grabbed their leashes. "Let's go, kids!" It felt good to have the decision settled. We stumbled out the door and took in the cold, clear night air. It was Ida's favorite time of day, her senses calmed by the darkness. She couldn't see any flying things or hear any loud noises. The woods were ours, safe and calm, and we were a family. Day by day, little by little, Ida Mae was different after that night. She lightened up a bit, and I stopped worrying so much about her. Analyzing her every quirk and behavior was put in the past. Eddie had a real partner again, and they fell into a routine, a comfortable companionship.

29

Just like Wolfie, Ida had no desire to stay outdoors all day like Eddie. She, too, preferred her cozy comforter to snuggle in while we were at work and school. At a book club meeting one night, I met a new friend Marie, and before long, we were walking our dogs together every morning either at the Goose Cove Reservoir, known as the "Rez," or at Good Harbor Beach. Marie's yellow Lab, Bailey, was a tennis ball loving *maniac.* In the summer, we'd meet at 5:30 a.m. at the beach. Ida Mae enjoyed chasing Bailey while he was chasing the ball. She couldn't care less about the ball. She liked banging into his side while he ran after the ball, nipping at his neck, bugging him, trying to distract him. Fat chance. His whole focus was on that ball. Ida would chase him right into the ocean.

Eddie would usually go about his walk, poking his nose into the sand dunes (or in the woods), uninterested in what Ida and Bailey were up to. Eddie wasn't ever one for the water. He was more of a hunter, an explorer. Chasing a ball must have seemed like a colossal waste of time to him. Eddie preferred the leftover trash that humans sometimes left behind, looking for scraps like in his old hobo days. It was a bit of a quandary, trying to keep him from getting sick on old bits of ham and cheese sandwiches.

Bailey and Ida Mae

In the winter, Ida had to wear a specially made coat, as greyhounds have very little body fat and need protection from the cold. Eddie, with his thick husky/shepherd-mix coat, looked at Ida in her purple coat (or her plaid one) and stared in disbelief. We once put a coat on Eddie on an especially cold morning and he stood stock still, not panting, eyes defiant. He wasn't going anywhere in a coat. I imagined him gritting his teeth, seething, and saying, "Get this thing off me. Now." Oh, that Eddie––he was so cute, even when he was pissed.

We had a girl dog and a boy dog once again and life felt settled. Some things did not change—Frank with his demanding job, my crazy work schedule, Sam's school and sports commitments during the week and on weekends. Busy, busy. Ida was still a scaredy cat but was calming much quicker when upset by some noise or flying object. Maybe she trusted us to protect her. And Eddie, well, he did not change at all.

Construction on new homes began in our neighborhood during our second year. Guys in pickup trucks came to the job sites each morning, loaded up with coffee and donuts. Eddie seemed to recognize this pattern. Workmen = Food. Eddie scoped out their routines for a few weeks. I'd watch him skirt by the workmen, not getting too close, but checking it out. *What was he planning?* It wasn't too long before I found out.

One morning as I was getting ready to leave for work, I see a Dunkin' Donuts box with a dog's body headed up the driveway. There were four or five donuts in it, a nice mix of jelly, sugar, and chocolate. Eddie's hobo instincts had kicked in, and he was robbing the construction workers of their morning sustenance. He had taken their mug-up. Another afternoon, I see a pizza box with a dog's body coming up the driveway with half a pizza in it. Pepperoni! Eddie was generous. He didn't just take the food and eat it, he took the boxes with the food in it and brought it home to us, to share with the family. Kind of like that turkey carcass from our first Thanksgiving with him. His antics were too funny, but I had to put a stop to the stealing.

I leashed him and dragged him with me like a naughty preschooler. I approached the work crew, and ratted on Eddie, advising them to keep an eye on their meals or Eddie would pull a Robin Hood and take them. Eddie was a sneaky thief, but I knew his intentions were good. He also couldn't hide his guilty-looking face. The guys had some laughs and a declaration of, "And here we've been blaming Teddy all this time of hoarding the goods!" *Geesh, Eddie.* He had somehow gotten the guys to blame one of their own.

The next few years were uneventful and life went on. We hadn't had any veterinary emergency room visits in a long time. Eddie had occasional playdates with his old pal, Steve, and Sam pretty much claimed Ida as her own.

She would swaddle her in blankets like a little baby, tucking her in, cooing to her. Sam would feed Ida pizza, holding onto the slice while Ida gently and delicately used her little front teeth to tear small pieces away from the crust. It was hysterical to watch her eat pizza that way.

Eddie remained "garbage dog," eating with abandon, so much so that he had to be watched the day before and the day of trash day. His old hobo habits were hard to break. He would stay outside for hours, sometimes making nests in the leaves, snuggling in for naps, no matter the season. We would give him rides to Steve's, and I think he finally understood that he didn't have to walk there. I was glad that he had stopped wandering so much and that I didn't have to worry about him.

30

About four years into having Eddie, he started to develop some strange habits. I once came home to find Eddie standing in a corner of the living room, his head against the wall. I called to him, but he didn't move. I knew he could hear me because he was giving me the side eye and panting. It was as if he had forgotten how to move his legs. *What was going on?* I went to him and gently turned him so he could move away from the corner. He seemed confused. How long he had been standing there? After hugging him, giving him a treat and water, both dogs went outside. He seemed okay. But this event stayed with me. It was so strange. The pacing began soon after. Endless pacing and circling in the house. A call to Vet Donna was in order.

It was the year 2001, and Frank and I had entered marriage counseling. We were trying to hang on to something good that we'd once had, though there was only a glimmer of that good remaining. We had been married seven years and things weren't getting, or feeling, any better. We were more like roommates, and I expected more out of our union. Dealing with Eddie's new issues made it easier to keep ignoring what was really going on; our marriage was headed to the end. We had only gone twice to our therapist when 9/11 happened. It seemed that everything started to "happen." We got caught up in the feeling of that period in time when the mantra of "life is too short" became a reason to stay and concluded that our marriage wasn't that bad. We shelved the counseling and decided we could do without it. We were doomed.

Eddie continued to pace the house, treading a circle from the kitchen to the living room, out into the hallway, through the den, and back into the kitchen. There was no end to it. All night long we would hear him begin to pace, the "click, click, click" of his nails on the kitchen floor, then nothing as he went through the carpeted living room, the "click, click, click" through the hallway, then silence through the carpeted den, only to start the clicking of his nails

through the kitchen again.

The only way to stop it was to pen him into one carpeted room where he would eventually wear himself out and collapse into a fitful sleep. When the pacing first started, I would check him all over, looking for something painful that was irritating him. There was nothing. He was still eating and drinking normally—no issues with his stomach. It was baffling. Vet Donna ran a series of blood tests, and there were no real abnormalities. It was determined that he was having some sort of "doggie dementia," and there wasn't much we could do about it. *Dogs get dementia? How could that be?*

We were told that dogs can develop canine cognitive dysfunction syndrome, which is a degenerative brain disease similar to Alzheimer's in humans. This explained how he was "trapped" in the corner that day and the relentless pacing. Vet Donna put him on some medication, hoping to calm the urge to pace.

Not long after beginning the medicine we were out for a short walk when on our way back he just keeled over onto his side, right there in the middle of the street. It was like seeing a cow tip over. Eddie had fainted. It was so bizarre. He recovered quickly, shook himself out of it, and was able to walk home. I called Donna right away, and she said that the medication had most likely lowered his blood pressure, therefore causing the fainting spell. No more of that medicine for Eddie. The medicine really didn't slow down his pacing much anyway, so we had to come up with another strategy. Donna suggested acupuncture, which she could do at our home. I was up for any solution, so we arranged for a visit.

This was new territory for me. *A dog having acupuncture?* I had taken Ida Mae to Dr. Ramsey, our chiropractor, for her track-related injuries to her spine even though up until Dr. Donna suggested it, I had not heard of dogs being treated by chiropractors. Dr. Ramsey also treated horses (so cool!) and was an accomplished rider.

Ida's treatments had been successful, giving her great relief from a bad shoulder that caused her to limp occasionally. Ida would stand in the exam room, nose dripping, while Dr. Ramsey used the activator (a gun-type device that makes a loud snapping noise, sending painless shock waves into the spine) up and done her neck, spine, and hips. She would sometimes do her knees. I was hesitant at first with the whole gun-type thing and the noise it made, since Ida Mae seemed to have PTSD from her racetrack days, but it didn't seem to bother her and after the treatments she was always better, a spring in her little doggie steps. Having had such a positive experience with Ida, I knew that we had to try the acupuncture for Eddie.

When Donna arrived, I had penned Eddie into the den and had a blanket ready for him to lie on. I'm sure he was alarmed at the sight of Vet Donna. *What is **she** doing here? She knows where I live??* He started to pant with anxiety, but Donna was sure and steady, a comforting presence. She took out her box of acupuncture needles and sat down on the floor. I sat down next to her and lured Eddie over with hushed tones and kisses. He wasn't having it. He looked like he wanted to bolt, staring at the door.

He started to try and pace in the small space of the room. I brought out the ammunition of freshly cooked bacon strips and gently took him by the collar. He stood on the blanket, eating the bacon, but with suspicion in his eyes. He eventually lay down. As Donna began to place the tiny needles into certain areas of Eddie's back and hips, he went into a trace. He stared off into space, calm, not panting, mouth closed. His nose began to drip. I have always thought of a dripping nose as a good thing. It's like the body becomes so relaxed that everything in the dog's system relaxes and flows freely. Eddie never once tried to move and he never cried out in pain. It really made a difference, and for the time being, it allowed him a respite from the exhausting pacing.

Unfortunately, the effects were short-lived and only lasted a few hours after a treatment. We had Vet Donna do this a few more times, always with good results, but sadly, always temporary. There wasn't much to do but to watch him and make sure that he didn't hurt himself. We surmised that he was about ten years old by then, but we really had no idea.

We started to talk about euthanasia. This is never an easy discussion to have about a beloved pet. We were trying to take it day by day, and if he got worse or seemed tortured, we would make the decision then. This was a depressing time. Ida studied him and lay by his side whenever he'd finally come to a stop. We went for long rides in the good weather, windows down, fresh air swirling through the car. Eddie would relax then, unable to pace, distracted enough to enjoy the time.

31

One day when I came home from work, I called for Eddie and he didn't appear. *Hmm.* I went inside to let Ida Mae out and continued calling his name. My next move was to call Steve just in case Eddie had made a trip to Rockport. He hadn't done that in a long time, but I was getting concerned. "Eddie's probably just on one of his little jaunts," I said, my voice a little shaky, trying to make light of it to Steve on the phone. He could tell I was nervous. He knew about Eddie's dementia. We hung up with the promise to call each other as soon as Eddie turned up. He was out there somewhere.

Frank and Sam eventually returned home, and we all started looking for him. We took turns going further up the road, into the woods near our house, and even had Ida along, hoping she might catch his scent, lead us to him. Nothing. After a few hours, it was dark. We started to fear the worst. With few street lights, our neighborhood was quite dark at night. The woods surrounding us filled with the echoes of our voices. Our flashlights were now out, and we continued calling and calling. My first instinct was that maybe Eddie had gone off to die. This was an ancient, unproven theory, dogs going off alone to die, but it felt that way. Where else could he be?

I went back to the house with Sam, our spirits defeated, but Frank would not give up. He decided to go further up the street, deeper toward the thicker, undeveloped woods. It was October, dark and chilly. We were losing hope that we'd find him. I made a call to the police to check if anyone had found a confused dog while Frank continued the search. No one had reported a lost dog. I left a message for the dog officer, but I didn't have much faith that he had been picked up. We lived in a secluded, small, wooded area. We had no need for any regular dog officer visits. There weren't many people living near us at the time. It seemed hopeless.

Sam and I were in the house when suddenly we heard Frank yelling. "I found him! I found him!" We both rushed out, scrambling into the street. We could barely see Frank, and he was hard to understand. He was gasping for breath. When he stepped into the lone streetlight, there was Eddie, in his arms. They were both covered in mud, all four of Eddie's legs and Frank's legs up to his knees. Eddie weighed at least fifty pounds. It was a struggle for Frank to carry him, but Eddie couldn't walk.

"Where in the world did you find him?" I exclaimed in horror. It took Frank a minute to muster the breath to tell us the story. He had just completed a dog rescue triathlon.

"I heard a dog barking, very faint, very far away. It was so quiet up there at the end of the road, and as I stopped calling for him and really listened, I heard the bark. I knew it had to be Eddie. So, I started to follow the sound, using my flashlight to guide me through the woods." Frank thrust Eddie into my arms, desperate for a break, bending over and grabbing onto his knees for support. He limped with us back to the house.

I was stunned. Sam grabbed lots of towels and a blanket, and we rushed Eddie into the den. We knew that he had been outside a long time and he was very cold. Sam and I started to clean the mud off and wrap him in blankets, hugging and kissing him. We held him tight to warm him, me crying like a fool, so happy to see him.

Here is what you need to know: Frank saved Eddie's life that night. Frank didn't just go into the woods, a flat, easy walk. He went down the side of a very steep incline, in the pitch black, with only a small flashlight. The hill was heavy with underbrush, thorny branches, and rutted with thick roots. He followed the sound of Eddie's barking until he found him, all four legs stuck in the mud up to his chest, howling his head off. Eddie was crying for help. Frank had to pry him out of the mud while sinking into it himself, holding the flashlight in his mouth.

Realizing that Eddie would never be able to make it up that steep, wooded hill, Frank had carried him, hauling him up with all his might, all the way out of the woods. Frank is only five foot eight. He is not a big guy. But that night, his heart made him stronger and braver than he himself could only imagine. Frank was exhausted, muddy, and upset. An immediate hot shower was in order. He needed to warm up, too.

Sam and I continued to tend to Eddie, feeding him bits of American cheese and lots of water. He was going to make it. Ida came over to Eddie and gave him a little kiss. She circled the three of us, whining a bit with her tail wagging a mile a minute.

It was such a relief to find him, but we also knew that this was a life-changing event. Eddie's roaming days were over. We could not leave him outside unattended any longer. Our hobo dog would have to have his routine curbed. I was saddened, knowing that his judgment to stay safe had been broken and that his life would never be the same.

Vet Donna made a house call the next day to check Eddie's health after his harrowing experience. She, too, could hardly believe this fantastical story of Eddie and Frank. However, she also confirmed our theory that he had most certainly become confused, possibly on his way to Steve's, through the woods. He could've died that night, alone, and we may never have found out what happened to him. He had also started to have small seizures, which were frightening to witness. Out of the blue, he would start howling then slump to the side, staring off into space, unable to hear us, his brain breaking down. We were slowly losing him.

Eddie needed a grand sendoff—a day to take him and Ida Mae out in the car for a ride to all his favorite places. He would love to hit the drive-thru at Dunkin' Donuts for some munchkins and McDonald's for a burger. Stop by the bank and the drugstore drive-thrus for extra doggie bones. I wanted to take him to the woods and the beach, take him to see some of his

doggie buddies...and Steve. In other words, I wanted to give him a farewell tour.

I dreaded seeing Steve and his wife, Judy. Who wants to see someone's heart break? But I knew that we had to let them know. My mind had accepted that it was time to let Eddie go. He was suffering. The pacing, the confusion, the seizures that Donna said would only get worse. Locking him in the house every day seemed cruel, detaining him like a criminal. We would become his jailers—again.

Unfortunately, Frank was *not* ready, and he would not agree to a planned euthanasia day. He had grown attached to Eddie, and since the rescue in the woods he had developed deeper feelings for him than he ever had before. Trying to convince Frank that this was best for Eddie was pointless. Reasoning that we couldn't think about our own pain now, that we had to think of Eddie, wasn't working.

Frank just couldn't do it. He had my sympathies, but I was frustrated that I was alone in my decision. It was only a matter of time, and that time came quickly, accelerating the inevitable whether we were ready or not.

32

Early in the morning on November 12, 2001, two months and one day after September 11, an American Airlines plane crashed into a neighborhood in Queens, New York, killing all 260 people on board, including five people on the ground. It was all over the morning news, having occurred at approximately 9:15 a.m. It seemed as if everyone in the United States was on edge, having just experienced the pain and suffering of the unspeakable events of September 11. I wasn't working that day, and for whatever reason that I cannot remember, Frank hadn't left for work yet. We were glued to the TV, our coffee going cold in our hands.

As I watched the news, numb and scared that we could be under a terrorist attack again, I heard a bang and then a crash. Eddie was having a seizure in the hallway. He started to howl like crazy, sending Frank flying down the stairs. Eddie's tongue was flapping in his mouth, and his eyes were glazed and wide open.

This seizure was the worst one yet, and I was furious. I glared at Frank. "Is this what you wanted? For Eddie's life to end like this?" I wished I could take back those words. I knew they really hurt Frank. But I'd had a plan. I had wanted Eddie to go out peacefully and blissfully unaware of his impending death. And Frank wouldn't let me. And now this was how it was going to end.

After a quick call to Donna, she arrived within minutes. Eddie was still on his side, panting and occasionally barking and barking. Frank would try to calm him, but it was like trying to lasso a thunderstorm. We had no control over what was happening and we couldn't stop it.

After Donna examined him, she gave us the bad news, news I'd already known would be coming for weeks. Eddie's brain was deteriorating, and she didn't see him coming out of this seizure with his wits intact.

It was over. Though heartbroken, I desperately wanted to put him out of his misery. Maybe I also wanted to be put out of the misery and pain of watching this dog suffer.

Ida Mae was standing by, her eyes wide with alarm, her tail frozen still. Vet Donna was in our house. Something was gravely wrong. She knew.

Together Frank and I slid Eddie from the hallway onto the carpet of the dining room. I led Ida over to where Eddie was lying, urging a goodbye. She gently licked his terrified face. He didn't seem to acknowledge it. I was sobbing by then. I looked up at Frank who was standing in the doorway. We nodded to each other and gave Donna permission to put Eddie to sleep.

Eddie was howling in a confused, agitated state when Donna slowly slipped the needle into Eddie's back leg. He calmed almost immediately, with no additional pain. He didn't even flinch. I apologized to him over and over, telling him how much I loved him and would miss him. He was gone in a minute. Quiet. Final. Gone.

I will always be grateful to Vet Donna. She took such good care of Eddie from the start, through all his crazy injuries and his quirky personality. Eddie was no longer suffering, but we all were mourning, in great pain at his loss.

Sam was in her senior year at boarding school, and I called her later to break the news. She wasn't surprised, as she knew his days were numbered, but it was painful to tell her over the phone and not be able to hold her as she cried. She asked after Ida Mae, who was snuggled up beside me, trembling a little, knowing in that innate way that animals do that something intense and serious had happened to Eddie. I sob while writing this chapter as if it happened yesterday.

Frank disappeared upstairs, saying he had to take a shower, had to get to work. *Work?* I knew that he was likely sobbing quietly in the shower, heartbroken to have lost his buddy he had just rescued from the woods only a few short weeks before. I also felt horribly guilty for what I had said to Frank in the heat of the moment. I knew that I would have some serious apologizing to do, but I wasn't sure it would help.

I regret those words that I said to Frank immensely, and I hope that he knows just how sorry I am. Our marriage was in serious trouble and here was proof: we couldn't even console one another. He was going to go to work and leave me alone. He didn't even think to stay home after such a painful event.

Vet Donna kindly took Eddie's body to her office to arrange for cremation. We carried him out to her vehicle together, wrapped in his favorite blanket, the weight of his body like a warm, precious stone. I will never forget Donna's kindness and compassion.

His ashes were returned within a week or so. When we divorced a few years later, I left his ashes with Frank. It was the right thing to do. I think they are still in the attic of our old house, the one we built together while dreaming of a future. I have Ida Mae's and Wolfie's.

Our Eddie was now released at last to roam throughout the Universe, throughout the world, with no restrictions, no human rules, no pain or suffering. He was truly free. He will always be missed.

Epilogue One

I have been blessed to have had many dogs in my life, and even though each one has had their own quirks and personalities, Eddie's story was by far the most compelling. I have thanked him numerous times in my heart for trusting us, for sharing his hobo ways, for letting us experience a dog who was like no other. I hope that you have enjoyed his story and will pass on some of his exploits for people to marvel at and appreciate. Eddie didn't know what a gift he was to the world. I can only hope that in telling his story, I am showing him the love and admiration that he deserves.

A hobo lifestyle is not one that I would wish for any domesticated animal. Even though it made for an incredible story, I feel saddened that Eddie had to fend for himself for so long. Somewhere along the way, a human or humans had hurt him, driving him into the gray and isolated days of being a hobo, of becoming that lost dog. Shame on anyone that injures or sends fear into an animal's tender heart. Animals are loving and innocent, trusting and precious.

Thank you, Eddie, for finding us and showing us that every dog needs love...and a home. And please, support your local animal shelters!

Epilogue Two

In August of 2018, as I was completing this book, I happened upon the obituary of Steve Davis. He had died on July 20, 2018. He was eighty-eight. I hadn't seen him in many years but still had hoped to one day show him the book and his role in it. I cried me a river reading that he had died, my eyes and heart swollen with missed opportunities. I had been thinking about him lately, and how I should look him up. I really wish I had listened to my intuition. I regret that I did not see him. The only consolation was that he was now with Eddie once again.

Through Facebook, I reached out to Steve's daughter, Jill, not knowing if she would remember me, much less respond. I thought I had completely missed my window since he had died in July. Any services were surely done by now. However, Jill told me that no services had been held, and she invited me to a gathering in her dad's honor coming up *that very Saturday.* She too remembered Eddie. He had never been forgotten by Steve. My luck had turned.

I was able to see Steve's widow, Judy, which was incredible. We were able to talk for quite some time. I hadn't seen this woman in twenty-five years (she's eighty-four), but not only did she remember me, she also remembered Eddie and all of his adventures. She said Steve talked about him all the time. It was overwhelming.

She also mentioned how her brother Roger, a retired Rockport police officer, had been the officer on duty the night that Wolfie was hit and killed by that car. *Judy's brother* was the one who had been so kind to me and wonderful in my unbelievable grief during that time. I never knew this until that day. *How could I not have known??* And here he was at the gathering!

I introduced myself, and we had a warm conversation. He told me that even though he didn't quite remember that particular night, he remembered the many dogs (and cats) killed by cars until a leash law was put into place in Rockport. He'd had many painful situations with pet owners, devastated at their loss. Many hugs and heartfelt thanks later, we parted ways with a promise that he'd get a free copy of this book.

When I left Frank in 2007, I moved back to Rockport and rented a tiny house on this unfortunately named side road called Timer Way. My new address was 2 Timer Way. A woman going through a divorce with that street address. *Ugh.* The upside were my new neighbors, a lovely couple who lived behind me with their young son.

One sunny afternoon, the wife, Laura, asked to speak with me about something important. She was wringing her hands with anxiety. "Do you know who my husband is?" I stared at her blankly. I had no idea who *she* was, much less her husband. This was odd. She was clearly uncomfortable. She continued with a gush of words. "His name is Jay. He hit and killed your dog when you used to live here a long time ago. He thinks you hate him...do you?"

We both stood stock-still. I was a bit stunned. Ten long years later, the man who'd hit Wolfie became my neighbor when I returned to Rockport during my divorce.

Laura and I went together to talk with him, and I reassured him that I held no ill will. I did not remember him (I had never met him in person) or even his name. A lot had happened in those ten years. What I *did* remember was his pain-filled phone call to me, and how truly sorry he had been for breaking our hearts. His empathy is what I remember to this day. We became good friends, and I enjoyed their friendship while I lived in that house until 2008.

Time really does heal, though the memories will never fade. I wanted to include these amazing events that transpired many years after Eddie's death, if anything to show that we are all interconnected. Judy and I now email each other and stay in touch. I haven't seen Jay and Laura since the late 2000s, but I will find them and send them all a copy of this book when it is published along with Judy, Frank, Dr. Donna, and Officer Roger Lesch. Sam will get her own special copy. Had I published it earlier in my life, this epilogue would not have blossomed into a healing end to this wonderful story about Eddie. Many thanks for reading his story.

ACKNOWLEDGMENTS

My sincerest gratitude to the members of the
Finish Line Writers Group
in my hometown of Gloucester, MA.:
Sandra Williams, Cindy Schimanski, Jane Keddy, John Mullen,
Cindy Hendrickson, Dan Duffy, and Barb Boudreau.

This book became the best version of itself with your
constructive criticism, positive feedback, and countless reviews.

Special thanks to Cindy S. for bringing me onboard,
just when I thought my creative life was over.
A very special thank you to my dear friend
Sandra Williams
for her sound advice, editorial skills, cheerleading, and teaching!

Milton Keynes UK
Ingram Content Group UK Ltd.
UKHW050802110923
428451UK00008B/43